SchoolSafe, StreetSafe ... ..., strategic view
with tactical strategies that you can share and practice with your children.
Just like everything else, discussing safety with your child needs to be an
ongoing dialogue not a one-time event. In *SchoolSafe, StreetSafe*,
Dave Kovar has developed some of the principles of *Black Belt Excellence*
into a practical guide for helping keep your family safe.

Modesty

Courtesy

Integrity

Perseverance

Courage

Indomitable Spirit

Hello!

ALTHOUGH THERE IS A LOT OF VIOLENCE in modern society, there is plenty we can do to minimize the odds of it happening to our children. Can a parent take every precaution possible to keep his family safe and still have his child suffer violence? Of course. However, with the right preparation, the right training and the right mindset, the odds will be strongly stacked in your child's favor.

An ounce of prevention is worth a pound of cure certainly applies to keeping our families safe. *SchoolSafe, StreetSafe* will help you train your child in strategic self-defense to feel more confident and empowered. Your child will communicate more confidence in the way she carries herself. Because bullies and predators usually approach children who appear vulnerable, hesitant or fearful, they will be less likely to single out your confident, empowered child.

There are conflicting theories as to when parents should begin to discuss real-world dangers with their children or if the topic should even be broached.

My take is that real-world dangers need to be discussed, but that the discussion should be age appropriate and introduced over time.

The overriding theme should be empowerment-based education not fear-based education. If you keep your child in the dark regarding safety issues, she can grow up naïve and be easy prey for predators. Whereas, if your consistent message is to "beware of strangers because there are a lot of bad people out there that want to hurt you," your child could grow up being overly fearful. This fear does not make your child safer. In fact, being overly fearful puts her more at risk.

The key is to discuss real-world, age-appropriate dangers in a calm, matter-of-fact fashion. Explain to your child that while there are bad guys out there, the majority of people they meet are good—but to be safe, there are certain guidelines that they should always follow.

Happy parenting!

Dave Kovar

Your Most Important Role *6*

Principle 1: Create safe habits *8*

Principle 2: Be aware, but not on guard *12*

Principle 3: Trust your intuition *16*

Principle 4: Take immediate action *20*

Principle 5: Learn from your and others' experiences *24*

Principle 6: Communicate with confidence *28*

Principle 7: Follow the five steps of bully prevention *32*

Principle 8: Dispel the myth of not talking to strangers *36*

Principle 9: Know who to ask for help *40*

Principle 10: When in doubt, get out *44*

Principle 11: No! Go! Yell! Tell! *48*

Why Your Child Needs Martial Arts *52*

Keeping It Simple *55*

About the Author *56*

Your Most Important Role

THE MOST IMPORTANT ROLE YOU WILL EVER HAVE is that of parent. Parenting can be extremely rewarding, but it's extremely challenging, too. Just when you think you have it figured out, something happens and it's back to the drawing board.

Ben Zoma, an early spiritual sage, often asked his students, "Who is a brave person?" Zoma described "a brave person" as "someone who is smart enough to be afraid, but does whatever needs to be done anyway."

To me, "being afraid" means that certain things are to be taken seriously. Parenthood is a real responsibility. Like it or not, we're responsible for helping to shape our child's life. We should not take this lightly.

Sow a thought, reap an action.
Sow an action, reap a habit.
Sow a habit, reap a character.
Sow a character, reap a destiny.

The above quote, attributed to Ralph Waldo Emerson, is one of my favorites. First and foremost, a parent's job is to do his best to raise his child to become a confident, healthy, happy and contributing member of society. And, in order to do this, parents need to help their children think in proactive, positive ways and develop strong self-images that will guide them through rough times.

The following *Parenting Guidelines* are designed to support your and your child's success.

You have probably heard most of these guidelines before. Most of them are common sense. However, knowing *what* to do and understanding *how* to do it are often two separate challenges. *SchoolSafe, StreetSafe* unites the *what* with the *how* for a logical, easy-to-use guide to parenting.

As you read, you might think that I'm exaggerating the importance of being positive with your child. Guilty as charged! In my experience of working with thousands of parents over the course of more than thirty years, rarely have I come across parents who are too positive with their children. I have, however, frequently seen parents spend way too much time criticizing and being negative with their children. At the other end of this spectrum, though more rare, are parents who believe their children can do no wrong. Both approaches are off kilter.

SchoolSafe, StreetSafe teaches positive, logical and effective parenting and communication skills in an intuitive format so that you will be able to begin to apply them immediately.

We're all busy. Even with the best of intentions, days or weeks might slip by in which we haven't used any of our parenting tools. If these tools make sense to you, you might try calendaring them into your phone or computer, even setting the alarm clock on your phone as a reminder or writing yourself notes placed in strategic locations.

Family Safety Principle 1

Create safe habits.

While most of us know how to live a safe life, we're not always aware of what we know. As parents, it is important to be conscious of what we know and to teach our children to be mindful, too. Awareness is the first step to safety.

To keep your family safe doesn't require that you lock them in the house and not let them out. On the contrary! Once you're aware of what you know about staying safe and put this simple knowledge into action, you will be giving your family more freedom than ever.

You create safe habits by doing what you know you should do. You help your child to create safe habits by teaching her to avoid potentially dangerous situations in the first place.

Knowledge

Safety

Wisdom

Protection

Intelligence

Description

Years ago, a man walked into my martial arts school to ask about lessons. He was sporting a black eye, stitches and a fat lip. It was pretty obvious that he'd been in a fight and wanted to learn to protect himself.

He told me quite candidly that he needed to learn self-defense. When I asked him why, he said that every time he went into this certain bar, he got into a fight. I responded, half jokingly, by telling him not to go to the bar in the first place. He literally slapped himself on the forehead and, with a startled look, said, "I never thought of that. What a great idea!" To me, this seemed obvious but, until I mentioned it, he had never thought of avoiding the potential for danger.

You'll be surprised how much you know already about safe habits. The following examples illustrate this point:

- Wear a seat belt
- Lock the car and house doors
- Get cash inside a store, not at an outside automated teller
- Fill up on gas in a good area of town during the day
- Shop with a friend
- Park in well lit areas
- When shopping, park as close as possible to the store with your car door facing the store

Pretty basic stuff that every adult should know, right? Do you follow these rules? Remember that creating safe habits doesn't mean you are being paranoid but that you are being smart and stacking the odds for safety in your favor.

Once you realize how much about safety you already know and recommit yourself to practicing safe habits, teach your child to do the same thing. Again, teaching your child to create safe habits requires an ongoing conversation. A one-time discussion isn't enough. Discuss the importance of avoiding potentially dangerous situations with your child frequently. The Socratic method works best. Teach your child by asking questions rather than by lecturing her.

Tool 1: Here's the big question—what potentially dangerous situations do you need to keep your child from getting into in the first place? Ask your child to name some dangerous situations that she should avoid. Your questions can guide her to discover the following scenarios and more.

Next, ask your child why she should avoid those situations & what the potential dangers are. Remember, don't scare her. Empower her. Remind her that if she creates safe habits, chances are, she will be just fine. Create a curfew and stick with it unwaveringly. Nothing good happens after curfew.

Family Safety Principle 2

★

....

Be aware,
but not on guard.

Being aware of potentially dangerous situations is not the same as being on guard. Being aware means to pay attention to what is going on around you, to exercise your peripheral vision that takes in the details of your surroundings, and to notice when something is not quite right or is very wrong.

Awareness

Responsiveness

Vision

Alertness

Attention

Description

Teaching our children to be aware should be empowering not scary. Arm your child with the gift of awareness. Discuss being aware of dangerous situations frequently. The possible dangerous scenarios will change as your child grows. Continue the dialogue throughout your child's growing years.

To be aware is neither to be on guard or its opposite, to be naive. Being aware is a lot like being a good driver. A good driver sees the big picture rather than narrowing his focus to one aspect of driving. Through relaxed, soft concentration a skilled driver puts his attention wherever it is most needed while still keeping his eye on the road and his surroundings.

An experienced driver neither expects to get into an accident nor does he rule out the possibility of an accident. He follows the rules of the road and doesn't overreact or underreact to his environment. If something were to occur on the road, the defensive driver trusts his instinct and skills to respond correctly.

Similar to the defensive driver, you can teach your child to be aware of his surroundings but not be excessively fearful. With this mindset, he can safely go about his business. He can be confident that, if something comes up that needs his immediate attention, his intuition will let him know.

We've all seen both on guard and naive drivers. They're scary! They over-compensate, overreact or neglect to respond to the conditions of the road. They create dangerous situations.

Tool 2: Once you are aware of how you are regarding safety, you can adjust it (if needed) to help your child be healthily aware but not on guard. Ask yourself where you fall on the safety scale:

- Are you more cautious and fearful that you should be? (Paranoid)

- Are you not cautious enough? (Naïve)

- Are you aware, but relatively free from over-worrying? Your answer is important because your child will adopt a similar mindset. Our children imitate how we are, as well as what we do. Also, your answer will make you aware of any changes you need to make regarding how you teach your child to drive his own life safely.

This awareness extends beyond being aware of potentially dangerous situations to being aware of others' goodness and the beauty of life, too. Team up with your child to notice how many good things are happening—acts of kindness, creativity, the beauty of nature, etc.

Family Safety Principle 3

★

....

Trust your intuition.

We all have had gut feelings about a person, place or event which we should have heeded, but didn't. Fortunately, most of these incidents were probably not life threatening. Can you think of a time when your instincts didn't seem logical, but were absolutely correct? Of course, you can. We've all had this experience.

Intuition

Instinct

Listening

Responsiveness

Honor

Description

Our intuition is always right in two important ways. It's always in response to something. And it always has our best interest in mind.

Listening to your intuition seems simple but it isn't always easy. As a matter of fact, many of us have been taught to ignore or stifle our intuition. There is often no logical explanation for what intuition is guiding us to do. We're used to feeling that we have to substantiate our decisions with hard facts for them to be viable. But intuition doesn't work that way. It's usually only after we listen or don't listen to it that we see exactly why our instincts made sense. If you have been taught to stifle your intuition then you're in danger of teaching your child to stifle her intuition and this puts her in danger.

Please note that your intuition or instinct is your innate knowing, your awareness on a deep level that keeps you and your child safe. Intuition is very different than are triggers. Triggers are incidents to which you have a deep psychological, emotional and, sometimes, physical reaction, based on your past. Reacting to triggers usually creates dangerous situations, whereas listening to intuition protects us from danger.

It is important that we teach our children to honor their feelings about circumstances and people. Listen to your child with your full attention. Encourage your child to talk about it. If someone makes your child feel uncomfortable, tell her that you're glad she told you and that you want her to bring these things to your attention.

Tool 3: Make a game of honing your child's intuition by constantly looking for teachable moments. Movies, stories and even television shows can be full of great lessons that you can discuss with your child. Everyday holds many real-life opportunities to teach your child to trust her intuition, too. The key is to ask your child frequently what she observes about other families, people and situations. Not only will she love the fact that you're curious about what she sees and the way she sees it, you'll be able to help her hone her intuition and to validate it with a few simple questions about her feelings and observations.

Family Safety Principle 4

★

....

Take immediate action.

Teach your child to be proactive under pressure and take immediate action. Usually this action is to leave the scene of trouble immediately.

Action

Immediacy

Bolt

Run

Description

Let's imagine the worst-case scenario for a moment. Your child finds himself confronted with a hostile situation. He has tried to diffuse the situation by practicing safe habits and being aware of his surroundings but still hasn't been able to avoid a confrontation. Aggressive action must be taken immediately. He should leave the scene quickly, if at all possible.

Leaving a dangerous situation quickly is called **bolt and run**. The idea behind bolt and run is to avoid putting yourself in a situation worse than the one you're already in.

Although there are times when your child needs to stand up for himself, dangerous situations are not those times. When it comes to imminent danger, your child needs to know how to bolt and run. It's survival, at that point.

In law enforcement, *crime scene 1* is where the incident starts. And *crime scene 2* is wherever it ends up. *Crime scene 2* is always worse than *crime scene 1*. Leaving the scene quickly will help your child remove himself from danger and avoid being a victim in *crime scene 2*.

Tool 4: Role-play with your child by setting up different scenarios to act out. Have him help choose the scenarios. For example, you can pretend to be a strange adult who approaches him at the park and forcefully says, "Hey kid, come here right now."

Family Safety Principle 5

★

Learn from your
and others' experiences.

We're all human and we all make mistakes, including our children. No one is perfect, but as long as we approach life as learners, we'll keep progressing. The trick is to teach your child to learn from her and others' mistakes and not repeat them.

Progress

Learn

Examine

Observe

Evaluate

Practice

Implement

Teach

Description

Learning from history keeps us from repeating it. Take a moment to think of times in the past when you unnecessarily put your safety at risk. What can you learn from this experience? How could you have handled this situation better? What steps can you take to ensure that this will not happen to you again? This will help you examine your mistakes in a new light... to learn from them. Then you'll be able to do this with your child.

It's important to remember that self-defense defies logic. Everyday someone somewhere effectively diffuses a potentially dangerous situation. Everyday someone somewhere effectively fights off and breaks free from a violent attack. How? She has what is referred to as the not-me mindset. She has decided that she will not become a victim. This is what we want to try to instill in our children as we teach them simple self-defense strategies, including learning from their and others' mistakes.

Tool 5: Ask your child to think of times when she put her own safety at risk unnecessarily. What did she learn from this experience? How could she have handled this situation better? What steps can she take to make sure that this won't happen again? Also, anytime you hear of something negative happening to someone else ask your child (if the topic is age-appropriate), "How could this have been avoided?"

You may not always come up with clear and decisive answers to every question. By having this dialogue frequently you help your child pick up clear, useable distinctions that can help her to respond better in the future. You are teaching her critical thinking or how to have the not-me or "safety" mindset.

Family Safety Principle 6

....

Communicate
with confidence.

The FBI did a study several years ago entitled, *The Three Stages of Assault*. In this study, the FBI uncovered the fact that most predators follow a basic pattern of attack.

First, they select a victim. Next, they test the victim for perceived vulnerability. Finally, they commit the physical assault.

With this in mind, the first step is to figure out how to minimize the risk of your child being selected in the first place. We already know that teaching our children to practice safe habits is the number one most important thing we can do to help them stay safe. But, in and of themselves, safe habits are not enough.

Inevitably, there will be times when your child's path might cross that of a predator. For this reason, you need to teach him how to develop the habit of communicating confidence in all of his actions, even when he doesn't feel confident. Be aware that the average bad guy doesn't have a back-up plan, but he does have an alternate victim. By teaching your child to communicate more confidently, you dramatically reduce his chances of being selected as a potential victim in the first place.

Eye Contact

Body Language

Voice

Confidence

Power

Strength

Action

Safety

Description

There is probably nothing more important for your child's safety than teaching him to carry himself with confidence. The three primary indicators of confidence are:

- **Body language** can either send the message that you're likely to be a passive, easy target or it can tell a potential attacker that he'd be better off picking someone else.

- **Making eye contact** sends the message that you're aware that the predator is there and that you're not likely to be a good target.

- The third step is **Tonality**. It isn't what you say, it's how you say it. Saying "Back off!" with authority has much more impact that saying it in a weak voice.

Assertive body posture, making eye contact and using strong tonality combine to make a strong statement to the attacker that he would be better off choosing someone else.

Tool 6: Team up with your child to practice the **PushoverKid/SuperKid drill**. First have him stand with slouched shoulders, his head down and his eyes looking towards the floor. This is **PushoverKid**. Ask him how he feels when he stands like that. Chances are that he'll tell you that he doesn't feel very good or confident.

Next have him pull his shoulders back and puff out his chest, bring his head up and chin in and have him make clear eye contact straight at you. This is **SuperKid**. To dramatize the effect even more, have him ball his hands into fists and rest them on his hips just like **Superman**. Ask him how he feels then. Chances are that he'll feel much more empowered. Although this is an exaggeration it gets the point across—appearing and acting confident is the first step to becoming more confident.

Family Safety Principle 7

★

....

Follow the five steps
of bully prevention.

Bullying has always been a serious issue for children. It is estimated that nearly forty percent of children have reported bullying and a large percentage of those children say it happens every day. What can we, as fathers, do to minimize the chances of our children being bullied? First and foremost, teach your child to ask an adult for help when she needs it. And if the problem is ongoing, your child can ask for help in advance of the actual bullying to prevent the situation from unfolding in a negative way.

Happy

Healthy

Mind

Words

Legs

Ask

Defend

Description

Before we get into specific strategies to prevent bullying, let's not forget that by simply following the guidelines laid out to you in *15 Powerful Tools for Successful Parenting* and *HealthierKids, SmarterKids* you will be going a long way to keeping your child safe from being a target of bullying.

This is because healthy children brought up in a loving atmosphere who have a high level of self-esteem are naturally less likely to be bullied in the first place. It is important that your child feels comfortable talking to you about anything. Frequently remind her that she can talk to you about anything. When she does want to talk to you about a sensitive issue make sure not to jump all over her or to discount her feelings. Otherwise, she'll quit talking to you about sensitive subjects. Remember that as an adult, someone calling your child a name might seem trivial but it can be traumatic. Just being there to listen will go a long way in keeping your relationship strong with your child.

The traditional, misguided way of dealing with a bully is to bring your child into the backyard to teach her how to punch. Although there is a lot of value in teaching your child actual self-defense skills, dealing with a bully involves a lot more than knowing how to throw a right cross. In our martial arts schools, we teach the **Five Steps of Bully Prevention**:

Step 1 – Use your mind. Teach your child to think ahead about all the things she can do to stay safe.

Step 2 – Use your words. Teach your child to use her words to talk her way out of trouble. In many cases, responding to a bully with eye contact and a confident voice takes some of the wind out of the bully's sails. After all, it's no fun bullying someone who won't let you push her around or who does not seem to be bothered by it.

Step 3 – Use your legs. Teach your child to walk (or run) away from trouble when words aren't working. This applies any time she is confronted by someone who is being mean to her and whom she doesn't know, and who she'll probably never see again. She could be at a park, mall, fair, sports field, etc.

When using her words isn't working and she feels a fight coming on and if she feels that she can get away, then she should get away...even RUN!

Step 4 – Ask for help. Teach your child that it is okay to ask for help if she is afraid or feels threatened. This is very important. Most kids don't want to be a tattletale. They are afraid that if they tell a parent or teacher about a bully or troublemaker that the other kids will make fun of them. Asking for help in advance might be the solution. Remind your child frequently that it is okay to ask for help. Assure her that her safety is important to you and her teachers.

Step 5 – Defend yourself. Teach your child that no one has the right to physically harm her. If she has had done everything within her power to avoid a confrontation, then she has the right to defend herself. Please understand that it's important to teach your child to be 100% against fighting. But if her back is against the wall and she has no choice, then your child should be 100% for defending herself.

It's amazing to me that just the simple act of being prepared to defend yourself can often keep the fight from ever happening. In martial arts we call it practice the fight so that you don't have to.

Tool 7: Have you child memorize the **Five Steps of Bully Prevention** by having her hold out her hand with her fingers spread. As she recites each rule, she brings one finger in to slowly making a fist. As she finishes the fifth step and closes her hand into a complete fist, have her say loudly, "Defend yourself!" and punch into the air.

Family Safety Principle 8

★

....

Dispel the myth of not talking to strangers.

Teaching your child not to talk to strangers is a completely abstract concept that is difficult for your child to understand because the child gets mixed messages. For example, if a woman in the grocery store checkout line asks your daughter for her name and she doesn't reply, often the parent will chastise his daughter for being rude and ask her to tell the nice lady her name.

Wisdom

Awareness

Care

Goodness

Description

I've given literally hundreds of school talks on this subject and am amazed at what I hear from students when I ask them what a stranger looks like. Generally speaking, children describe a stranger as being big and scary, wears sunglasses and has a lot of tattoos and a beard.

I tell the kids that a stranger is simply someone that they don't know until their parents introduce them. Then I remind them that most strangers are good people who have no interest in harming them. But, unfortunately, there are a few individuals who aren't good people. So we need to take certain precautions. I also tell them that there is a difference between niceness and goodness. Just because somebody is nice to you doesn't necessarily mean that he's good person.

Tool 8: Team up with your child to help her hone her instincts about who she should and should not talk to by discussing real-life situations. Asking your child questions will help her understand what degree of interaction is appropriate with an adult. For example, after you walk out of the grocery store where you had your child introduce herself to the person in front of you, you can ask her, "That was a nice man, wasn't he? If I weren't around and he asked you to go somewhere with him, would you do it? Why not?"

Family Safety Principle 9

....

Know who to ask for help.

The thought of getting lost is scary for people of all ages. For children, it can be especially frightening. Many parents give their children the well-intended advice, "Don't talk to strangers." However, the whole concept of strangers is confusing and misleading for your child.

As we discussed in Family Safety Principle 8, a stranger is simply someone that your child doesn't know until you have introduced him. If your child is not to talk to strangers, what does he do when he's lost or separated from the family? If he is afraid to ask for help, he'll withdraw and become more frightened and confused. It is a known fact that predators look for lost, lonely, confused or weaker victims.

Ask

Moms

Grandmas

Uniforms

Workers

Description

If your child is lost or needs help for some reason, should he wait for some-body to come up to him to see if he needs help? Or should he ask someone for help? Most definitely, teach your child to ask for help.

Remember that the odds of your child approaching a predator to ask for help are pretty rare. Conversely, the odds of a predator approaching your child if he appears lost are much greater. For this reason, it's crucial to teach your child to approach someone to ask for help when he is lost or needs help. But who?

Let's assume there are lots of grown-ups around but he doesn't know any of them and there are no law officers to be seen. Who should he ask?

Moms with children should be his first choice. Their strong maternal instinct kicks in immediately, as they picture their own children lost. Usually, a mom will do everything in her power to help your child.

Next on the list is someone that looks like a grandma for the same reasons. After that, any person in uniform…the UPS person, mail carrier… pretty much anyone in uniform will do. And if your child can't find anybody who fits the above descriptions, he should look for someone working. Also, remind your child to stay put. Wandering off to look for you or his mom will only confuse him and make him more difficult to find.

Teaching your child to be assertive and to approach adults is very empowering and can go a long way towards making him feel more confident.

Tool 9: When you're out and about with your child, ask you child to be aware of the people around him and choose someone he'd ask for help. Do it often and in many different types of places. And team up with your child to practice actually approaching an adult he doesn't know.

Game 1. Whom should I ask for help? Sit in the park with your child and have him tell you about all the people he sees. Ask him which person he would approach for help and why. If he gets it right, let him know. If he could have made a better selection, tell him why and start over again.

Game 2. Excuse me, do you have the time? Go to a public place someplace where there are a lot of people. Have your child pick out someone he feels comfortable approaching. Have him walk up to that person and simply ask for the time.

Family Safety Principle 10

★

....

When in doubt, get out.

Every responsible parent tries to teach his child good manners. We teach our children to be especially polite to grown-ups. We teach them to follow the rules, listen to their teachers and obey authority. While these are all important things, we should also teach them that, if they ever feel uncomfortable around an adult, it's okay to risk offending the adult. When in doubt, get out, even if it might offend someone.

Intuition

Action

Safety

Back off

Get Away

Leave

Description

Being easily in awe is really about appreciating the time and effort your child
Teach your child that her safety is more important than any adult's feelings.
Your child should be taught never to worry about hurting someone's feelings
if she feels that her safety is at risk. Better to risk offending an adult by telling
him to back off or get away—even if it becomes clear later on that the adult
had no ill intent—than it is to go along with an adult's seemingly innocent
request because she didn't want hurt his feelings. When in doubt, get out!

Teach your child that "when in doubt, get out" means that she always
trusts her intuition...that intuition is:

- That feeling she gets about places or people that she just can't quite
  explain.
- When someone gives her the creeps or when being somewhere makes
  her feel uncomfortable.
- Her radar that warns and protects her from danger.

Teach her that she should always listen to her intuition. This means that
if she ever feels uncomfortable with someone or someplace she should leave
and find help, even if it hurts another's feelings. Have an ongoing dialogue
about intuition and the importance of listening to it. Praise your child when
you see her listening to her intuition. Frequently remind your child that it's
okay to risk hurting people's feelings if it means keeping herself safe.

Tool 10: Teach your child the statement, "My safety is more important than their feelings." Have your child say, "My safety is more important than their feelings," aloud and with confidence again and again. Have your child yell it. Join in. Yell with your child, "My safety is more important than their feelings!" Present different scenarios and play-practice listening to intuition, leaving and getting help, with your child.

Family Safety Principle 11

No! Go! Yell! Tell!

NO! GO! YELL! TELL! is a universal, easy-to-remember phrase that applies to virtually every situation regarding your child's safety. Whether it be the site of an accident, a bully, or a house on fire, NO! GO! YELL! TELL! applies.

No!

Go!

Yell!

Tell!

Description

NO! Teach your child that it's okay to say "No!" to a person (or a situation) with whom he doesn't feel comfortable.

GO! Teach your child to leave the scene immediately when he feels physically threatened or in danger.

YELL! Teach your child to draw attention to the threatening situation. Teach him to yell "Fire!" rather than "Help!" (Most anything is better than "help.") For example, "There's a stranger after me," "He's not my father" or "This kid is trying to beat me up" are much better than just yelling "Help!"

TELL! Teach your child to tell a safe adult what happened no matter how embarrassing, scary or trivial the incident seems.

NO! GO! YELL! TELL! is a vital tool for your child, especially when it comes to lures. Explain to your child that lures are tricks that people might use to get him to go with them when he knows that he shouldn't. Teach him that a good person knows that it isn't right to do this and would never ask him to come with him.

There are four classic lures. The first lure is the **Bribery Lure**. This is when someone tells your child that he will give him a toy or candy if he comes with him. The second lure is the **Job Lure**. This is when someone offers to pay your child money if he helps him with something. The third lure is the **Assistance Lure**. This is when someone asks your child for help. And the fourth lure is the **Direction Lure**. Do grown-ups ask kids for directions? No.

Tool 11: Role-play with your child. Pretend to be a stranger using the four lures and have him practice NO! GO! YELL! TELL!

Why Your Child Needs Martial Arts

THE BENEFITS OF ENROLLING YOUR CHILD in a martial arts program extend far beyond self-defense. Martial arts will help your child in nearly every aspect of her life. It will improve your child's health, fitness, athletic abilities, confidence, concentration and behavior.

Does this sound too good to be true? It's not. Many experts agree that martial arts are good medicine for the escalating childhood obesity, increased violence at school, and deterioration of the family structure.

There is a reason why Dr. Phil, Jillian Michaels (expert from the television show, *The Biggest Loser*), Tony Robbins, pediatricians, child physiologists and educators the world over all recommend martial arts as one of the most valuable activities in which your child can participate.

Confidence   *Composure*

Health   *Control*

Fitness   *Respect*

Strength   *Self-defense*

Flexibility   *Safety*

Endurance   *Success*

Athleticism   *Achievement*

Balance   *Goals*

Peace

The Benefits of Martial Arts

Self-Defense. The self-defense benefits of martial arts could be described as practice the fight so that you don't have to. As your child trains he will become more confident in his ability to defend himself. As this confidence increases the need to defend himself will decrease naturally because he will begin to carry himself in a more confident manner. He'll project confidence to everyone around him and will be less vulnerable to predatory behavior. Martial arts training includes strategic or preventative self-defense as well as physical self-defense. Your child will learn how to recognize potentially dangerous situations and how to avoid confrontations.

Athletic Enhancement. There is a reason why every professional sports team in every major sport supplements their training with martial arts. Martial arts training offers several advantages. It is amazingly effective in enhancing general coordination because it uses every part of the body in a balanced way. Upper body, lower body, right side, left side, forward movement, lateral movement and rotational movement are all included in martial arts training.

Fitness. Fitness has three components: strength, flexibility and endurance. Martial arts training demands a balance between the three. Therefore, a child who trains in martial arts will find her weakest areas greatly improved. Because of her greater balance of strength, flexibility and endurance your child will be less likely to injure herself while participating in other athletic activities.

Health. While martial arts training improves health for people of all ages, it is especially effective for children. It's great exercise and it's fun so kids don't mind doing it. And part of martial arts training includes discussing diet and lifestyle habits so children who grow up training develop healthy habits that stick with them for life.

Concentration. Very few activities engage the mind, body and spirit more than martial arts. Because of this a child's ability to concentrate is greatly enhanced by his martial arts training. He'll bring this ability to concentrate to other activities, too.

Respect and Courtesy. Martial arts techniques are, by nature, designed to injure others when applied. Because of this, martial arts instructors greatly stress the importance of respect, courtesy and restraint. It has been proven time and again that children who are skilled in martial arts tend to be extremely respectful, considerate and composed.

Confidence. Martial arts training always increases a child's confidence for two specific reasons. First, there are no bench sitters. Every child participates and competes against her own potential rather than against the other students. Second, martial arts training is built on the concept of setting your child up for success by giving her a series of realistic, short-term goals that she can attain quickly while keeping her focused on an exciting long-term goal. Each time she experiences success her confidence improves until she begins to believe that she can accomplish just about anything with hard work and dedication.

Keeping It Simple

MORE AN ART THAN A SCIENCE, raising children is both challenging and incredibly rewarding. Each child comes into this world with his own agenda. Oftentimes our children throw curves at us that we never saw coming and, when that happens, it is hard to know exactly what to do.

I'm reminded of a story I once heard about a famous landscape architect, a master. He traveled the world creating amazing gardens and landscapes at prestigious locations. On days when he felt particularly challenged, he would pull out a mysterious piece of paper from his pocket, glance at it, nod, fold it back up and get to work with renewed inspiration and energy, resulting in another masterpiece. People were astounded by his brilliant designs that would seem to appear from thin air after he studied that piece of paper.

Eventually, the master died. His curious colleagues approached his widow and asked to see that mysterious piece of paper as they were convinced it contained the secret to his success.

After much to-do, she allowed them one glance at the old slip of paper. As they gathered around, she carefully unfolded the paper. They looked at the writing. It simply said, "When laying sod, always put the green side up."

I love this story! It reminds me how easy it is to overcomplicate things, especially parenting. In my experience, the answers to most parenting challenges are in these *HealthierKids, SmarterKids*. We only have to remember to call upon them in times of need.

I hope you'll find *HealthierKids, SmarterKids* to be a valuable resource for years to come.

Dave Kovar

TAUGHT BY HIS PARENTS TO HAVE RESPECT for health and fitness at an early age, Dave Kovar has spent his adult life perfecting his approach to better physical, mental and emotional fitness.

A father of two, Dave holds the rank of black belt in ten different martial arts disciplines. In one of those disciplines, he has achieved a seventh-degree, which has earned him the title of "Kyoshi."

Dave Kovar is known in the martial arts world as the "Teacher's Teacher." Since 1978, Dave has helped over 25,000 students of all ages develop their character and fitness through martial arts instruction through his *Kovar Satori Academy of Martial Arts* schools and the hundreds of martial arts schools with which he has consulted. Over the years, Dave has carefully developed a system that helps his students apply the mental aspects of martial arts to excel in many areas of their lives.

The Martial Arts Industry Association (MAIA) presented Dave with its "2010 Lifetime Achievement Award" in recognition of his teaching abilities. This prestigious award has also been won by Chuck Norris and other martial arts luminaries. In 1992, the United States Martial Arts Association (USMA) honored Dave as its "Martial Arts Instructor of the Year."

Dave Kovar continues to break new ground with innovations in the martial arts industry, including fitness, nutrition and character development. Revered for being a successful businessman, Dave is also a highly respected authority in optimizing personal fulfillment and in peak performance.